PRAYERS FROM THE ARK

Prayers

Illustrations by
JEAN PRIMROSE

FROM THE *Ark*

by
CARMEN BERNOS DE GASZTOLD

*Translated from the French
and with a Foreword and Epilogue by*

RUMER GODDEN

New York   THE VIKING PRESS

First published in France under the titles:
Le Mieux Aimé and *Prières dans l'Arche,*
1947 and 1955, Copyright Editions du Cloître
English text Copyright © Rumer Godden 1962

Viking Compass Edition
Issued in 1969 by The Viking Press, Inc.
625 Madison Avenue, New York, N.Y. 10022

SBN 670-21973-8 (hardbound)
670-00258-5 (paperbound)

Library of Congress catalog card number: 62-19610

Printed in U.S.A.

Some of these poems appeared in *McCall's*

Third printing June 1970

CONTENTS

Prayers from the Ark, which now includes the poems of a smaller book, *Le Mieux Aimé,* has had what could be called a hidden life, being published by the Éditions du Cloître, the private press of the Benedictine Abbaye Saint Louis du Temple at Limon-par-Igny, France, where the poet lives and works. Though they have gone through none of the normal commercial channels, they have sold over thirty thousand copies in France and, in a German version, are selling equally well in Germany and Austria.

I came upon them by accident and was instantly caught by their charm, but do not be alarmed; the charm has nothing to do with whimsy: Carmen de Gasztold has seen too much of the seamy side of life to be a sentimental animal lover—ironically, she has little use for pets. In her world a dog is to guard the house, a horse to work its strength out for its master, a pig to be eaten, and there is an economy and sense about her work that is typically French; it is the truthfulness of the prayers, especially as it re-reflects on us, unthinking humans, that causes pain.

When I resolved to try to translate them it was almost a detective work, both in London and Paris, to find the poet; even when I had traced her to the Abbaye in its wide, rolling green park, it took time to win her confidence and that of her nun advisers—a novelist does not, one might agree, seem a proper person to translate a poet. Nor were these easy poems; their very simplicity makes them difficult. The economy of words, the subtle play on the double meaning of some of them, the integral rhythm, have been almost impossible to catch, and there is in each some phrase or word that is utterly elusive.

How, for instance, in "The Lark," can one render in English the opening,

> *Me voici, ô mon Dieu,*
> *Me voici, me voici!*

with the insistent, shrilling sound of that French i-i-i? Or find a word, in "The Little Bird," for *intarissable*—"*cette intarissable musique*" that repeats the sound and meaning? All our corresponding words seem to be weighted with "sh." Or in "The Old Horse" replace that word *encense* in

> *Ma pauvre tête encense*
> *toute la solitude de mon coeur!*

which gives, in two syllables, the double picture of the old horse's swinging head and a censer swinging to "offer up" in the Catholic sense all that he has left, his loneliness? The dictionary translation of *encenser*, which, when used of a horse, means "to toss," is too young and gay.

I am unhappily aware that I have not come anywhere near the poems' original worth. Perhaps a better poet could have found better answers; I do not know. But I do know that I have seldom had more rewarding hours than those spent working over these poems, first at Stanbrook Abbey, here in England, then with Carmen Bernos de Gasztold herself in the Abbaye parlour, helped from behind the grille by the two nuns in charge of the Éditions du Cloître.

These poems are prayers, Catholic in origin but catholic also in the sense that they are for everyone, no matter of what creed. Carmen Bernos lives now in an atmosphere of prayer, more importantly of belief, but they have not been influenced by the Abbaye. She is too independent to be influenced by anybody; in fact, she likens herself to her own *Chèvre,* the wild goat, and a goat—besides being wild and free—is obstinate. Most of the prayers were written long before she came to the Abbaye, in a scant hard time in which she had to do uncongenial work in the laboratory of a silk factory near Paris—a time of enemy occupation, hunger, cold, frustration; yet it was then that she was able to find, in each of these workaday, infinitesimal, or unfavoured creatures, not only its intrinsic being but an unexpected grain of incense that wafts it up, consecrates it, and this in the most matter-of-fact way.

The Abbaye has only endorsed what she knew a prayer must be—if it is to have any meaning; not something dreamy or wishful, not a cry to be used in emergency, not even a plea, and not necessarily comforting. A prayer is a giving out, an offering, compounded of honest work and acceptance of the shape in which one has been created—even if it is to be regretted as much as the monkey's—of these humble things added to the great three, faith, hope, and love.

PRAYERS FROM THE ARK

Seigneur,
quelle ménagerie!

Lord,
what a menagerie!
Between Your downpour and these animal cries
one cannot hear oneself think!
The days are long,
Lord.
All this water makes my heart sink.
When will the ground cease to rock under my feet?
The days are long.
Master Raven has not come back.
Here is Your dove.
Will she find us a twig of hope?
The days are long,
Lord.
Guide Your Ark to safety,
some zenith of rest,
where we can escape at last
from this brute slavery.
The days are long,
Lord.
Lead me until I reach the shore of Your covenant.

Amen

N'oubliez pas, Seigneur,
que je fais lever le soleil!

Do not forget, Lord,
it is I who make the sun rise.
I am Your servant
but, with the dignity of my calling,
I need some glitter and ostentation.
Noblesse oblige. . . .
All the same,
I am Your servant,
only. . .do not forget, Lord,
I make the sun rise.

Amen

Il n'y a que Vous et moi
pour comprendre
ce que c'est que la fidélité!

Lord,
I keep watch!
If I am not here
who will guard their house?
Watch over their sheep?
Be faithful?
No one but You and I
understands
what faithfulness is.
They call me, "Good dog! Nice dog!"
Words. . .
I take their pats
and the old bones they throw me
and I seem pleased.
They really believe they make me happy.
I take kicks too
when they come my way.
None of that matters.
I keep watch!
Lord,
do not let me die
until, for them,
all danger is driven away.

Amen

. . .protégez de la pluie et du vent
mon petit nid.

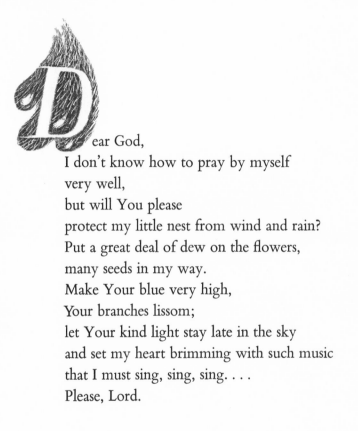

ear God,
I don't know how to pray by myself
very well,
but will You please
protect my little nest from wind and rain?
Put a great deal of dew on the flowers,
many seeds in my way.
Make Your blue very high,
Your branches lissom;
let Your kind light stay late in the sky
and set my heart brimming with such music
that I must sing, sing, sing. . . .
Please, Lord.

Amen

. . .mais une étincelle vivante
dans la douceur de Vos joncs. . .

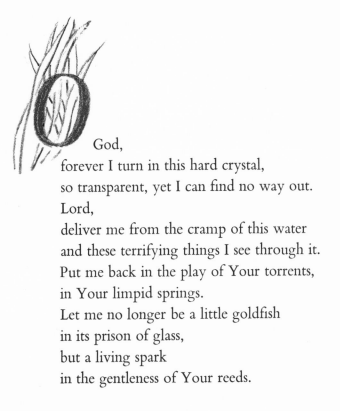

God,
forever I turn in this hard crystal,
so transparent, yet I can find no way out.
Lord,
deliver me from the cramp of this water
and these terrifying things I see through it.
Put me back in the play of Your torrents,
in Your limpid springs.
Let me no longer be a little goldfish
in its prison of glass,
but a living spark
in the gentleness of Your reeds.

Amen

Pourquoi m'avez-Vous fait si tendre?

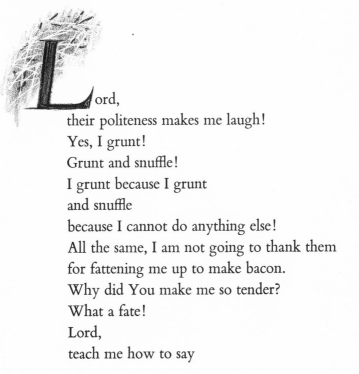

ord,
their politeness makes me laugh!
Yes, I grunt!
Grunt and snuffle!
I grunt because I grunt
and snuffle
because I cannot do anything else!
All the same, I am not going to thank them
for fattening me up to make bacon.
Why did You make me so tender?
What a fate!
Lord,
teach me how to say

Amen

Faites qu'il pleuve demain et toujours.

ear God,
give us a flood of water.
Let it rain tomorrow and always.
Give us plenty of little slugs
and other luscious things to eat.
Protect all folk who quack
and everyone who knows how to swim.

Amen

Mes sabots sont pleins de gambades. .

O God! the grass is so young!
My hooves are full of capers.
Then
why does this terror start up in me?
I race
and my mane catches the wind.
I race
and Your scents beat on my heart.
I race,
falling over my own feet in my joy,
because my eyes are too big
and I am their prisoner:
eyes too quick to seize
on the uneasiness that runs through the whole world.
Dear God,
when the strange night
prowls round the edge of day,
let Yourself be moved by my plaintive whinny;
set a star to watch over me
and hush my fear.

Amen

Me laisserez-Vous sans fin
retomber au creux des sillons,
pauvre oiseau d'argile?

I am here! O my God.
I am here, I am here!
You draw me away from earth,
and I climb to You
in a passion of shrilling,
to the dot in heaven
where, for an instant, You crucify me.
When will You keep me forever?
Must You always let me fall
back to the furrow's dip,
a poor bird of clay?
Oh, at least
let my exultant nothingness
soar to the glory of Your mercy,
in the same hope,
until death.

Amen

Faites que je trouve un beau chardon
et qu'on me laisse le temps de le cueillir.

O God, who made me
to trudge along the road
always,
to carry heavy loads
always,
and to be beaten
always!
Give me great courage and gentleness.
One day let somebody understand me—
that I may no longer want to weep
because I can never say what I mean
and they make fun of me.
Let me find a juicy thistle—
and make them give me time to pick it.
And, Lord, one day, let me find again
my little brother of the Christmas crib.

Amen

Que ma petite parcelle d'ardente vie
se fonde dans la grande activité communautaire. .

Lord,
I am not one to despise Your gifts.
May You be blessed
Who spread the riches of Your sweetness
for my zeal. . . .
Let my small span of ardent life
melt into our great communal task;
to lift up to Your glory
this temple of sweetness,
a citadel of incense,
a holy candle, myriad-celled,
moulded of Your graces
and of my hidden work.

Amen

Ne permettrez-Vous pas, un jour,
que quelqu'un me prenne au sérieux?

Dear God,
why have You made me so ugly?
With this ridiculous face,
grimaces seem asked for!
Shall I always be
the clown of Your creation?
Oh, who will lift this melancholy from my heart?
Could You not, one day,
let someone take me seriously,
Lord?

Amen

Le vent a peint ses fantaisies
sur mes ailes.

Lord!
Where was I?
Oh yes! This flower, this sun,
thank You! Your world is beautiful!
This scent of roses. . .
Where was I?
A drop of dew
rolls to sparkle in a lily's heart.
I have to go. . .
Where? I do not know!
The wind has painted fancies
on my wings.
Fancies. . .
Where was I?
Oh yes! Lord,
I had something to tell you:

Amen

Je me nourris de choses élevées. . .

Lord,
   I who see the world from above
   find it hard to get used to its pettiness.
   I have heard it said
   You love humble creatures?
   Chatter of apes!
   It is easier for me
   to believe in Your greatness.
   I feed on exalted things
   and I rather like
   to see myself so close to Your heaven.
   Humility!
   Chatter of apes!

Amen

Seigneur,
je ne suis que poussière et cendre!

ust and ashes!
Lord,
I am nothing but dust and ashes,
except for these two riding lights
that blink gently in the night,
colour of moons,
and hung on the hook of my beak.
It is not, Lord, that I hate Your light.
I wail because I cannot understand it,
enemy of the creatures of darkness
who pillage Your crops.
My hoo-hoo-hooooo
startles a depth of tears in every heart.
Dear God,
one day,
will it wake Your pity?

Amen

. . .je suis tout petit et très noir. . .

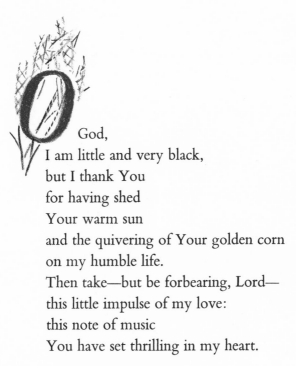

God,
I am little and very black,
but I thank You
for having shed
Your warm sun
and the quivering of Your golden corn
on my humble life.
Then take—but be forbearing, Lord—
this little impulse of my love:
this note of music
You have set thrilling in my heart.

Amen

Je ne demande rien à personne!

Lord,
I am the cat.
It is not, exactly, that I have something to ask of You!
No—
I ask nothing of anyone—
but,
if You have by some chance, in some celestial barn,
a little white mouse,
or a saucer of milk,
I know someone who would relish them.
Wouldn't You like someday
to put a curse on the whole race of dogs?
If so I should say,

Amen

*Je suis
comme un petit morceau
de cendre!*

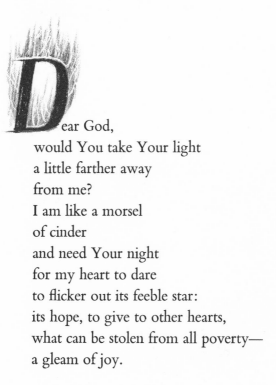

ear God,
would You take Your light
a little farther away
from me?
I am like a morsel
of cinder
and need Your night
for my heart to dare
to flicker out its feeble star:
its hope, to give to other hearts,
what can be stolen from all poverty—
a gleam of joy.

Amen

On ne m'a jamais rien donné.

am so little and grey,
dear God,
how can You keep me in mind?
Always spied upon,
always chased.
Nobody ever gives me anything,
and I nibble meagrely at life.
Why do they reproach me with being a mouse?
Who made me but You?
I only ask to stay hidden.
Give me my hunger's pittance
safe from the claws
of that devil with green eyes.

Amen

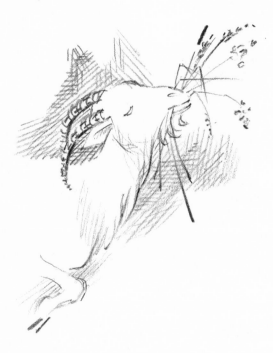

Pour qui seraient Vos montagnes
et ce vent de neige et de sources?

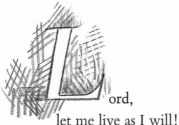 ord,
let me live as I will!
I need a little wild freedom,
a little giddiness of heart,
the strange taste of unknown flowers.
For whom else are Your mountains?
Your snow wind? These springs?
The sheep do not understand.
They graze and graze,
all of them, and always in the same direction,
and then eternally
chew the cud of their insipid routine.
But I—I love to bound to the heart of all
Your marvels,
leap Your chasms,
and, my mouth stuffed with intoxicating grasses,
quiver with an adventurer's delight
on the summit of the world!

                                        Amen

Je suis bien embarrassé de ma personne...

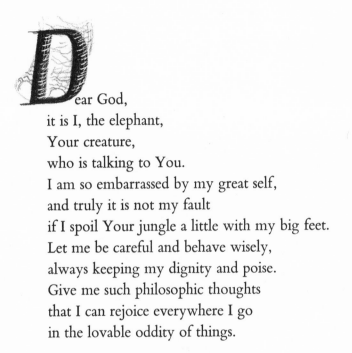

ear God,
it is I, the elephant,
Your creature,
who is talking to You.
I am so embarrassed by my great self,
and truly it is not my fault
if I spoil Your jungle a little with my big feet.
Let me be careful and behave wisely,
always keeping my dignity and poise.
Give me such philosophic thoughts
that I can rejoice everywhere I go
in the lovable oddity of things.

Amen

Mon Dieu, donnez-moi du temps.

ear God, give me time.
Men are always so driven!
Make them understand that I can never hurry.
Give me time to eat.
Give me time to plod.
Give me time to sleep.
Give me time to think.

Amen

Je suis la fable du monde!

Lord,
I am always made out to be wrong;
a fable to the whole world.
Certainly I hoard
and make provision!
I have my rights!
And surely I can take a little joy
in the fruits of all my work
without some sob singer
coming to rob my store?
There is something in Your justice
that I scarcely understand,
and, if You would allow me to advise,
it might be thought over again.
I have never been a burden to anybody,
and, if I may say so,
I manage my own business very well.
Then,
to the incorrigible improvidence
of some people,
must I, for all eternity, say

Amen

Un peu de patience,
mon Dieu,
j'arrive!

A little patience,
O God,
I am coming.
One must take nature as she is!
It was not I who made her!
I do not mean to criticize
this house on my back—
it has its points—
but You must admit, Lord,
it is heavy to carry!
Still,
let us hope that this double enclosure,
my shell and my heart,
will never be quite shut to You.

Amen

Je suis Votre serviteur inutile!

See, Lord,
my coat hangs in tatters,
like homespun, old, threadbare.
All that I had of zest,
all my strength,
I have given in hard work
and kept nothing back for myself.
Now
my poor head swings
to offer up all the loneliness of my heart.
Dear God,
stiff on my thickened legs
I stand here before You:
Your unprofitable servant.
Oh! of Your goodness,
give me a gentle death.

Amen

Je ne reviendrai plus dans l'Arche!

 believe,
Lord,
I believe!
It is faith that saves us, You have said it!
I believe the world was made for me,
because as it dies
I thrive on it.
My undertaker's black
is in keeping with my cynical old heart.
Raven land is between You
and that life down there, for whose end I wait
to gratify myself.
"Aha!" I cry. "*Avant moi le déluge!*"
What a feast!
I shall never go back to the Ark!
To the Ark. . .
Oh! let it die in me—
this horrible nostalgia.

Amen

Je suis la simple colombe!

he Ark waits,
Lord,
the Ark waits on Your will,
and the sign of Your peace.
I am the dove,
simple
as the sweetness that comes from You.
The Ark waits,
Lord;
it has endured.
Let me carry it
a sprig of hope and joy,
and put, at the heart of its forsakenness,
this, in which Your love clothes me,
Grace immaculate.

Amen

WHEN CARMEN BERNOS DE GASZTOLD was a child in her mother's tall house in Arcachon, she used to run down the flights of stairs so quickly that she really believed she was flying, a fitting belief for the poet who was one day to write "The Lark."

Arachon is in France, in the province of Bordeaux, a small town set between pine forests and the sea. On the father's side, the great-grandfather was Lithuanian, and this Slavonic blood seems to have mingled in his family the paradox of its dark melancholy and sparkling vivacity with the steady reserve of the provincial French. It was an unusual family, and, as Carmen Bernos says, not practical: Monsieur de Gasztold was professor of Spanish at Arcachon, but the household was overshadowed by his inability to make enough money to keep his growing family. Scheme after scheme was tried; he bought a machine for pleating cloth; then a button machine,★ but one after another the schemes failed. He was, too, often seriously ill, and then the younger children were sent away for the day to the Sisters of Saint Joseph, and for Carmen there began the terror and horror she always met when away from home. What to more ordinary people is simply sad, humdrum, or hard, to a poet can be excruciating. Carmen's first memories are of two cots, one red, one white; her sister

★ This gives me a fellow feeling with the poet. My father, too, bought a button machine, to make pearl buttons from the mother-of-pearl linings of the mussel shells that abound in the Brahmaputra River of Bengal. It might have made money, only no one ever found out how to separate the pearl from the shell.

Micheline in the white, uninhibitedly turning somersaults, while she herself crouched in the red one, peering through the bars, too afraid of doing something wrong to move. Trivial things happened that to her were searing. She saw a mistress put a donkey's head on a stupid child in class; worse, a nun once said to her kindly, "Now you are my little girl." "I am Maman's, Maman's," she had sobbed, terribly distressed. Still, there were compensations in being Carmen; Micheline had difficulty in learning to read; the younger Carmen, standing beside the teacher's knees, read the book—upside down.

There were five children, close as only children surrounded by an unsympathetic world can be. To the good people of Bordeaux, money was the measure of position, and these children, whom one can guess to have been beautifully mannered, delicate in thought and feeling, often suffered acutely from their father's lack of success. "Play by yourselves," their mother told them, and they grew up in a proud family solitude.

The eldest girl, Simone, succeeded in getting a post as a teacher in the Collège Sainte Marie at Neuilly near Paris, run by the famous Madame Daniélou under the guidance of the Jesuits. When Carmen was twelve, Simone persuaded Madame to take her small sister on a bursary, and for the rest of Carmen's school life the Collège provided everything; but she found the life of a boarding school terribly shut in; she could not sleep and was plagued by a bad memory which made it difficult for her to learn. In the end she gave up trying to get her diploma and felt she had failed Madame Daniélou. Yet it was the Révérend Père Daniélou who, some years later, published Carmen's first poems in the magazine *Études*.

Meanwhile at home things had grown steadily worse. Her father was in hospital and no longer knew his family, a great grief to Carmen, who did not understand he had gone out of his mind but thought that he had ceased to love them. If the house had not been Madame de Gasztold's, it would have been sold. At last Monsieur de Gasztold died. Childhood was over. At sixteen Carmen had to leave Neuilly and start to earn her living.

She began teaching children but was so shy that she walked round and round the pupils' houses, not daring to go in.

When war broke out she was a governess in Normandy but had fortunately come home to Arcachon for the baptism of the first of Simone's eight children. For a while she stayed on with her mother at Arcachon, but, having no means of living there, they were forced to go back to Neuilly, where they had a small apartment. They had to sell the mother's remaining jewelry to get there, and give up the house.

For seven years Carmen Bernos worked in a laboratory of an artificial silk factory, helping to support her mother and, in the years before the war ended, enduring all the hardship, lack of proper food and fuel, the restrictions, petty and big, of the German occupation, as well as the harassing days at the laboratory. Yet it was in this time that, one evening, as Carmen was writing to a friend, a poem suddenly came. "It was there—on the page," says Carmen. After that she wrote secretly, at every free moment, huddled in an old eiderdown to keep herself warm, choosing her ice-cold room rather than the one in which the family gathered around the one stove of the apartment. The poems poured out— all the poems of *Le Mieux Aimè*.

The war was over, but that brought no ease. In 1945 the mother died, and with her death the whole world seemed to fall to pieces. The Arcachon home was gone. Carmen had given up her work at the laboratory and was a governess once more in a French family at Lisbon. There a friend of the family, a Russian by birth, fell in love with the bewildered, homesick girl who was also extremely beautiful. Carmen Bernos is beautiful. Her head is as proudly set as the young Napoleon's in the painting; she is dark, with fine bones, and her brown eyes are so eloquent she hardly needs to talk. On the eve of the marriage Carmen, uncertain about her own feelings, broke the engagement. Then at last she found work she loved, teaching the kindergarten class of Sainte Marie every afternoon—she had thirty children to look after—but in an effort to help Micheline, who was in difficulties, she accepted the charge of teaching another class in the morning. For the delicate, highly wrought girl the strain was too much, and there was a breakdown, physical and mental, serious.

It seemed that there was no one to help at the moment of this illness, the brothers and sisters had troubles of their own, but a lifelong friend of the family's was a nun in the enclosed order of Saint Benedict, and now the Mother Abbess of the Community sent for Carmen and took her under her wing. Their well-known monastery in the Rue Monsieur in Paris had had to be given up, and they were now building the new Abbaye of Saint Louis du Temple at Limon-par-Igny, just south of Paris. Standing in a great park, the Abbaye, with its yellow stone walls, cloisters, great chapter house, fine staircase, guest parlours, and chapel, plain yet noble with its marble floors, stone vaulted ceiling, and exquisite modern stained glass, has been built by the community, using mainly workmen nobody else would employ. For more than four years the nuns nursed Carmen, keeping her on their farm and encouraging her to write; besides *Prayers from the Ark*, she has written other poems and several books for children. Everyone worked; indeed, the Abbaye might be the hive in "The Prayer of the Bee":

Que ma petite parcelle d'ardente vie
se fonde dans la grande activité communautaire
pour que s'élève, à votre gloire,
ce temple de douceur,
cette citadelle d'encens,
ce grand cierge cloisonné
pétri de vos grâces
et de mon obscur labeur!

Amen

A good atmosphere in which to get well, and Carmen Bernos was cured, but now, though she goes away to stay with her brothers and sisters, the Abbaye has become home and she lives and works "*dans l'ombre de l'Abbaye,*" as she puts it and is their cherished "child." Her room is in the Tower, the great old *colombier,* or dove house, recently made into an extra guest house; it is here that she writes, working meanwhile in the Abbaye library and as a fitter on the stained-glass windows with their jewel-bright colours.